ZEN CAT

ZEN CAT

concept by JUDITH ADLER

photographs by PAUL COUGHLIN

RODALE

Printed in China
Rodale Inc. makes every effort to use acid-free ∞ , recycled paper ♻ .

Book design by Maggie Hinders

Library of Congress Cataloging-in-Publication Data

Adler, Judith, date.
    Zen cat / concept by Judith Adler ; photographs by
Paul Coughlin.
        p.   cm.
    ISBN 0–87596–923–2 hardcover
    1. Cats—Pictorial works.   2. Photography of
cats.   3. Quotations, English.   4. Zen Buddhism.
I. Coughlin, Paul.   II. Title.
SF446.A45   2003
636.8'0022'2—dc21   2003011940

Distributed to the book trade by St. Martin's Press

2 4 6 8 10 9 7 5 3 1 hardcover

To all the magical, mysterious felines that so gracefully sat for Accidental Zen Master's camera long enough to be captured on film, so their mystical images could capture the mysteries of Zen.

To Jerry, Connie, Sabina, Nuna, and Aura. —P.C.

To Aunt Miriam, the greatest cat lover I know, thanks for your insight into the feline mind. To "Leo," the kitty loan shark, may your pawnshop be profitable. —J.A.

Acknowledgments

THANKS TO OUR BRILLIANT AGENT Susan Golomb for your guidance and inspiration, and to our lovely editor Margot Schupf for your wisdom, patience, vision and wit! Many thanks to Sara Sellar for your support, to Patricia Field for your guiding hand and artistic impeccability, and to Carol Gilmore for your mindful attention to detail. To our talented designer Maggie Hinders, thanks for your kindness, vision and endless creativity. Big thanks to Sabine Hrechdakian and Amira Pierce. "Toda raba" to the gang at Spectra Photo, particularly Josh Weiss, David Rajwan, Marti Andersen, Shalom Ben-Yosef, Roy Weiss, Zeke Rosenson, Diana Giraldo-Kurk, Derrick Edwards, Marilou Denusta, Gerald Bowens, Nataki Williams, Tort Prescott, Tina Rodriguez, and Bruce Ferguson.

Special thanks to KittyKind, the cat-rescue charity at Petco Union Square in New York City. Many of the cats photographed were saved from a sad fate by these wonderful, dedicated volunteers. The world is a better place for having Beverly Wilson, Marlene Kess, and Raven in it. To the Washington Square Animal Hospital, especially Dr. Ann Lucas, Dr. Kristin Kutscher, Joan Debellis. Fredi Grieshaber, Addie West, and Pat Fusco. Gratitude to Donald Williams, Jane and Robert Gordon (with fond memories of Cody), Leo and Sam Cohen-Gussack, and Terry Calway. Warm hugs to Courtney, James, and Nesta Brown.

To our soul friends and family, who helped out with the "purrfect" thing when we needed it most, thanks for being "cat-alysts" for this book. From the bottom of our hearts, our gratitude for always taking "paws" to offer love and support.

I purr, therefore, I am.

—ANONYMOUS

Introduction

Do not dwell in the past. Do not dream of the future.
Concentrate the mind on the present moment.

—BUDDHA

ZEN, LITERALLY TRANSLATED, MEANS "MEDITATION" which, in its purest form, involves nothing more (or less) than simply sitting, (preferably) motionless with (ideally) an empty mind concentrated on the present moment. Now think about a cat, focused, present, sitting stiller than a statue, meditating. What a perfect example: to be as still as a Himalayan, as present as a Persian, as one-pointed as a Russian Blue Point.

So, how did felines come upon their meditative mindfulness? Well, for one thing, they've had plenty of time to ponder the wonders of the world. Thought to be the first animals domesticated by man, the ancient Egyptians so prized the company of their cats they painted murals of them on the walls of tombs and often mummified them so they could join them in eternity. A wise friend of mine, a psychiatrist, spoke of cats being "bridges between heaven and earth" with a sense of them as furry little ambassadors from beyond. Cat lovers know the uncanny emotional perceptiveness of cats, their ability to offer comfort and share deep emotions at precisely the right moment. Cultivating this level of sensitivity, of mindful awareness of our own feelings and those of others around us, is something we can all take a lesson from. Anyone who has felt their sadness softened by the gentle stroking of a kitty's fur might suspect, as do I that cats are actually tiny love machines, with the quietly purring little motors to prove it.

> You could search the world over and never find
> anyone more deserving of your love than yourself.
>
> —BUDDHA

While dogs, generally speaking, are dogged in their unconditional love of their people, cats are "cat-alysts" for showing us how to love ourselves more. Cats exemplify a sense of self-contentment and satisfaction with their own company, enjoying life without the need for constant interaction and approval.

One moment in the presence of such present beings as felines says it all—they have no need to possibly even *consider* being anything other than the regal beings they are, as simply being their very own selves surely must be more than good enough. And, without pretense, it is. There is no doubt about how a cat feels about things, no games, no pretending, no lying about their own feelings to make people happy. They embody a sense of self-knowing, independent, self-contained little emotional units, enjoying the company of their "people" if, and when, they decide to. No chance that your cat's sticking around to hang out with anyone they don't enjoy being with—can you say the same of yourself?

> Consciousness is always open to many
> possibilities because it involves play.
> It is always an adventure.

> —JULIAN JAYNES

The Dalai Lama speaks of cultivating a child-like sense of wonder even as we develop a mature, benevolent heart. Within virtually every cat, there seems to exist an inner kitten that never grows up. Ever playful, cats express joy, lightheartedness and mirth, finding pleasure in the little things. They can chase a string, or even a shadow, for hours, jumping from pillar to post in search of a bit of fun. There are countless ways that cats amuse us with their antics, bring us joy and comfort and enhance the lives and in many ways just by doing nothing, they do everything. A favorite cat of mine spent entire days seemingly asleep, but I wonder if he wasn't actually dreaming up ever more daring high-wire routines, death-defying leaps of grace Barishnikov himself would envy. Just as a cat can spend countless hours following a twirling toy, when we take the time to really pay attention to our play, life becomes more fun. Recently a wise old cat taught to follow the graceful dance of light upon the walls of my bedroom. Finding my own inner feline, apropos of the Leo that I am, I now mindlessly follow the soothing rhythms of the intriguing patterns, watching as they shift and change with the passing light.

As T. S. Eliot said, "Teach us to care and not to care. Teach us to sit still." Cats certainly do that. And as we stalk that elusive quality of deep relaxation, perhaps we can calm our restless minds long enough to imagine that maybe, in our eternal search for peace, it's inside of us all along. It is that harmony, that delight, that tranquility we can find in the swish of a cat's tail, if only we're wise enough to catch the moment. As anyone who has ever been blessed enough to share life with a cat knows, nine lifetimes of love is never enough, and always plenty.

the
no-mind
no-thinks
no-thoughts
about
no-things

—BUDDHA

Paradise

is

where

I am

—VOLTAIRE

What is Buddha?

The cat is climbing up the post.

—PA-CHAIO HUI-CH'ING

Whatever interests, is interesting.

—WILLIAM HAZLITT

If we fail

to look after others

when they need help,

W H O

will look after us?

—BUDDHA

When you have developed

bodhicitta in your heart,

all the good things in life

are magnetically

attracted to you and effortlessly

pour down

upon you

like

rain.

—LAMA THUBTEN YESHE

I entered into my inward self and beheld with
the eye of my soul . . . the Light Unchangeable.

—SAINT AUGUSTINE

The truth

knocks on the door

and you say,

"Go away, I'm looking for the truth "

and so it goes

away.

— ROBERT PIRSIG

Teach us *to care* and *not to care*
Teach us TO SIT STILL.

—T. S. ELIOT

Things are entirely what they appear to be

and behind them . . .

there is NOTHING.

—JEAN-PAUL SARTRE

The only joy in the world is to begin.

—CESARE PAVESE

en **JOY** *ment*

is not a goal,

it is a feeling

that accompanies

important ongoing

activity.

—**PAUL GOODMAN**

Penetrating so many secrets,

we cease to believe in the unknowable.

But there it sits nevertheless,

calmly licking its chops.

—H. L. MENCKEN

A hand-rolled
Dumpling of
Heaven-and-earth;
I've gulped it down
And *e a s i l y* it went.

—DIM SUM ZEN

T   I   M   E

is the longest distance between two places.

—TENNESSEE WILLIAMS

God

made everything

out of nothing, but the

nothingness

shows through.

—PAUL VALERY

Cats don't belong to people.

They belong to places.

—WRIGHT MORRIS

When I play with my cat,

W H O   K N O W S   if I am not

a pastime to her

more than she is to me?

—MONTAIGNE

In the "Not Two" are
no separate things,
yet all things are included.

—SENG-TS'AN

Love's gift

cannot be **given**,

it waits

to be *accepted.*

—RABINDRANATH TAGORE

I love all solitary places, where we taste

The pleasure of believing what we see

Is boundless, as we wish our souls to be.

—PERCY BYSSHE SHELLEY

Action

should culminate in

WISDOM.

—BHAGAVAD GITA

The CAT

does not negotiate

with the mouse.

—ROBERT K. MASSIE

The PRESENT MOMENT is a powerful goddess.

—JOHANN WOLFGANG VON GOETHE

Don't listen to what they say.   G O   S E E .

—CHINESE PROVERB

A painting

of a rice cake

does not

satisfy hunger.

—ANCIENT SAYING

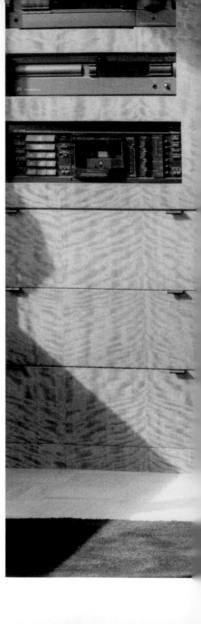

CATS,

by means of their whiskers,

seem to possess something like an additional sense:

these have, perhaps, some analogy to the antennae

of *moths* and *butterflies*.

—REVEREND W. BINGLEY

God gives E V E R Y bird its food
but He doesn't throw it in the nest.

—JOSHUA HOLLAND

There are only

two mistakes

one can make

along the road to truth:

not going all the way,

and not starting.

—BUDDHA

The aspects of things that are

most important for us

 are hidden because of their

simplicity and familiarity.

—LUDWIG WITTGENSTEIN

Attachment is the mind stuck to AN OBJECT.

—LAMA ZOPA RINPOCHE

The great charm of cats

is their rampant egotism,

their devil-may-care attitude

toward responsibility,

their disinclination to earn

an honest dollar.

—ROBERTSON DAVIES

We are

the mirror

as well as

the face in it.

We are

tasting the taste

this minute

of eternity.

—RUMI

The longer I live,

the more *beautiful* life becomes.

—FRANK LLOYD WRIGHT

The more you think of others,

the H A P P I E R you will be.

—HIS HOLINESS THE DALAI LAMA

I teach two things and two things only.

That is suffering
and the end of suffering.

—BUDDHA

Think with the WHOLE body.

—TAISEN DESHIMARU

Silence is the garden of meditation.

—ALI

Travel, for many of us,

is a quest for not just the unknown

but the unknowing.

—PICO IYER

Wisdom is sometimes nearer

when we stoop

than when we soar.

—WILLIAM WORDSWORTH

Even the

smallest feline

is a

masterpiece.

—LEONARDO DA VINCI

How many cares one loses

when one decides not

to be some *thing* but to be

someone.

—COCO CHANEL

The city of cats and

the city of men

exist one inside the other,

but they are not the same city.

—ITALO CALVINO

It's enough to make a

c a t laugh.

—PROVERB

With all your science

can you tell how it is,

and whence it is,

that *light* comes into the soul?

—HENRY DAVID THOREAU

Sometimes it proves

the highest understanding

NOT to understand.

—GRACIAN

When hungry, eat your rice;
When tired, close your eyes.
Fools may laugh at me,
but wise men will know what I mean.

—LIN-CHI

spontaneity.

The Tao's principle is

—LAO TZU

Learning is like a design in the *water*,

Contemplation like a design on the side of the WALL,

Meditation is like a design in STONE.

—ADEPT GODRAKPA

Z E N has nothing to grab onto.

—YING-AN

Even a cat is a lion

in her own lair.

—PROVERB

Photographs

FRONT COVER: Buster Bowersock; PAGE 2: Nesta Brown; PAGE 10: Kitten at KittyKind, New York City; PAGE 12: Charley Fogler in paper bag; PAGE 15: Mya Whitney's backyard cat; PAGE 16: Noodle Fineberg-Tobin; PAGE 19: Cat adoption at KittyKind, New York City; PAGE 20: Annabel August Schulz with Kiss-Kiss September Schulz; PAGE 23: Doc Carson; PAGE 25: Cat at doorway, Brooklyn Heights, New York; PAGE 26: Doc Carson by window; PAGE 29: Cat with Japanese screen; PAGE 30: Starbuck; PAGE 32: Buster of Aphrodisia, New York City; PAGE 35: Phyllis Levy's Pansy; PAGE 36: Butch the Ansonia Cat; PAGE 39: Doc with Carol Divine Carson; PAGE 40: Stanley-Thunder, the blue and white Sphynx; PAGE 43: Antique store cat, New York City; PAGE 45: Man with kitten at KittyKind, New York City; PAGE 46: Street performer's cat and dog, Paris, France; PAGE 48: Prrsia Coffey with gift; PAGE 51: Raspberry Zeitlin in drawer; PAGE 53: Peewee in window of Aphrodisia, New York City; PAGE 54: Toby Avery-Gross; PAGE 56: Layla Bell with Kwan-Yin; PAGE 58: Winston Roseman; PAGE 61: Rootbeer (Rooty) the Sable Burmese watching TV; PAGE 62: Lina Lett's Vergil; PAGE 64: Chloe Scott in basket; PAGE 67: Cat on Brooklyn Street; PAGE 68: Cat at the Hogan Gallery in Canyon de Chelly, Arizona; PAGE 71: Toby Avery-Gross with string; PAGE 72: Cat on cash register, New York City; PAGE 75: Chocolate Chip "Chipper" the Sable Burmese in mirror; PAGE 76: Poet Sabina Jacyna Roseman with Sebastian; PAGE 78: Cats for adoption at KittyKind, New York City; PAGE 81: Cat in cemetery, Jamaica, New York; PAGE 82: Boris Donaldson Carr, the Russian Blue kitten; PAGE 85: Hobbs Kreston in garden; PAGE 86: Cat at Café Reggio, New York City; PAGE 89: Trixie Lee of Chinatown, New York City; PAGE 90: Oswald "Waldo" with painting by Christopher Pugliese; PAGE 92: Freddywina Chanin-Greenberg in pearls; PAGE 95: Cat in front of copy of Michelangelo's David statue, Piazza Signoria, Florence, Italy; PAGE 96: Angela of the Washington Square Animal Hospital, New York City; PAGE 99: Madison Mastrangelo's Kozy; PAGE 100: Cat at newsstand, New York City; PAGE 103: Buster Bowersock; PAGE 104: Kiss-Kiss September Schulz jumping; PAGE 107: Peggy Sand's Roca cat, San Gimignano, Tuscany, Italy; PAGE 109: Bean Bowersock displaying his large paw; PAGE 110: Jack Fogler.

Photographs are by Paul Coughlin with the exception of pages 46, 68, 95, and 107, which are by Judith Adler. Photographs on pages 35 and 36 are by Paul Coughlin and Jim Dratfield, Petography Inc.

The painting by Christopher Winter Pugliese is courtesy of the Arcadia Gallery, New York City.

The KittyKind Cats are courtesy of the KittyKind Rescue Charity in partnership with the Mayor's Alliance for NYC Animals. Stanley-Thunder, Sphynx, is courtesy of Ben Munisteri and breeder: Arden Gatlin-Andrews, Angelfire Sphynx Cattery.